Smart About Sports

Meet the Astros

By
Mike Kennedy
with Mark Stewart

NORWOOD HOUSE PRESS

Norwood House Press, P.O. Box 316598, Chicago, Illinois 60631

For information regarding Norwood House Press,
please visit our website at: www.norwoodhousepress.com or call 866-565-2900.

Photo Credits:
    Getty Images (4, 7, 15, 21, 22), Associated Press (8, 12, 13), Icon SMI (16, 20), Black Book Partners (18, 23 top and
    bottom).
Cover Photos:
    Top Left: Topps, Inc.; Top Right: Aaron M. Sprecher/Icon SMI; Bottom Left: Ronald Martinez/Getty Images;
    Bottom Right: Topps, Inc.
The baseball memorabilia photographed for this book is part of the authors' collection:
    Page 6) Rusty Staub: Topps, Inc., Page 10) Jim Wynn, Cesar Cedeno, Larry Dierker & Nolan Ryan: Topps, Inc., Page 11)
    Craig Biggio: Fleer Corp.; Jeff Bagwell, Lance Berkman & Roy Oswalt: Topps, Inc.
Special thanks to Topps, Inc.

Editor: Brian Fitzgerald
Designer: Ron Jaffe
Project Management: Black Book Partners, LLC.
Editorial Production: Jessica McCulloch

LIBRARY OF CONGRESS CATALOGING-IN-PUBLICATION DATA
    Kennedy, Mike (Mike William), 1965-
    Meet the Astros / by Mike Kennedy with Mark Stewart.
        p. cm. -- (Smart about sports)
    Includes bibliographical references and index.
    Summary: "An introductory look at the Houston Astros baseball team.
    Includes a brief history, facts, photos, records, glossary, and fun
    activities"--Provided by publisher.
    ISBN-13: 978-1-59953-370-4 (library edition : alk. paper)
    ISBN-10: 1-59953-370-7 (library edition : alk. paper)
    1. Houston Astros (Baseball team)--Juvenile literature. I. Stewart, Mark,
    1960- II. Title.
    GV875.H64K46 2010
    796.357'64097641411--dc22
                                2009043049

Manufactured in the United States of America in North Mankato, Minnesota.
N147—012010

Contents

Words in **bold type** are defined on page 24.

The Astros celebrate their first trip to the World Series, in 2005.

The
Houston Astros

During the 1960s, the United States wanted to be the first country to send a man to the moon. Astronauts soon became America's biggest heroes. In 1965, they started training at a new base in Houston, Texas. That same year, Houston's baseball team changed its name to Astros. The team has been flying high ever since.

Once Upon a Time

The Astros joined the National League (NL) in 1962. For their first three years, they were named the Colt .45s after a gun that was famous in the Old West. The Astros have always put great players on the field. Rusty Staub and Nolan Ryan are just two of many.

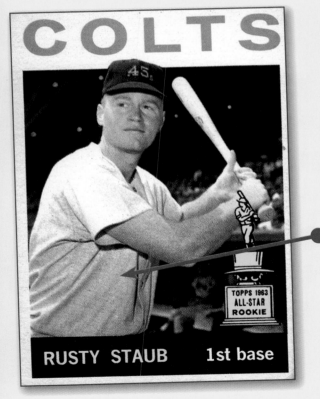

RUSTY STAUB   1st base

Nolan Ryan stares in at a hitter as he throws a pitch.

Houston's players and fans get ready for the 2005 World Series.

At the Ballpark

The Astros play their home games in one of baseball's most beautiful ballparks. It opened in 2000. The Astros' stadium has a roof that opens and closes. There also is a train that runs along a track in the outfield. The Astros used to play in the Astrodome. It was the first stadium with a roof.

Shoe Box

The cards on these pages belong to the authors. They show some of the best Astros stars ever.

Jim Wynn

Outfielder

• 1963–1973
Jim Wynn was not very tall, but he hit a lot of home runs. His nickname was the "Toy Cannon."

Cesar Cedeno

Outfielder • 1971–1981
Fans loved to watch Cesar Cedeno. He was the second player ever to hit 20 home runs and steal 50 bases in the same season.

Larry Dierker

Pitcher • 1964–1976
Larry Dierker threw hard and never seemed to get tired. He was the first Astro to win 20 games in a season.

Nolan Ryan

Pitcher • 1980–1988
Nolan Ryan's fastball sometimes reached 100 miles per hour. The "Ryan Express" pitched a no-hitter for Houston in 1981.

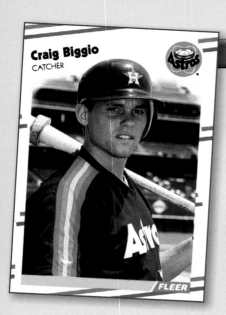

Craig Biggio

Second Baseman

- **1988–2007**

Craig Biggio played catcher, second base, and the outfield for the Astros. He had 3,060 hits in his career.

Jeff Bagwell

First Baseman • 1991–2005
Jeff Bagwell was one of the team's greatest hitters. In 1994, "Bags" batted .367. In 2000, he scored 152 runs.

Lance Berkman

First Baseman • 1999–
Lance Berkman batted both right-handed and left-handed. In 2006, he set a record for "switch-hitters" with 136 **runs batted in**.

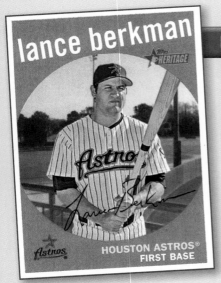

Roy Oswalt

Pitcher • 2001–
Roy Oswalt was a tough pitcher who hated to lose. Oswalt won 20 games two years in a row for the Astros.

11

ABC's of Baseball

In this picture of Hunter Pence, how many things can you find that start with the letter **H**?

See page 23 for answer.

Brain Games

Here is a poem about a famous Astro:

There once was an Astro named Cruz,
Who simply hated to lose.
His hitting and running,
And throwing and cunning,
Meant other teams never could snooze.

Guess which one of these facts is **TRUE**:

- Jose Cruz's son (Jose Jr.) played for the Astros in 2008.
- Jose once hit a ball through a hole in the roof of the Astrodome.

See page 23 for answer.

Jose Cruz watches the ball after a hit to the outfield.

Junction Jack
always points
the Astros in the
right direction.

Fun on the Field

One of the best things about going to an Astros game is watching their mascot, Junction Jack. Junction Jack is a seven-foot jackrabbit. He spends time on the field and in the stands. Sometimes he visits schools around the city.

The team's stadium is built near Houston's old railroad station. A railroad junction is where train tracks meet. That explains the *Junction* in Junction Jack.

On the Map

The Astros call Houston, Texas home. The players come from all over the country—and all over the world. Match these pitchers who each won 20 games or more in one season with the places they were born:

 Joe Niekro • **21 wins in 1979** • **20 wins in 1980**
Martins Ferry, Ohio

 Mike Hampton • **22 wins in 1999**
Brooksville, Florida

 Roy Oswalt • **20 wins in 2004** • **20 wins in 2005**
Kosciusko, Mississippi

 Larry Dierker • **20 wins in 1969**
Hollywood, California

 Jose Lima • **21 wins in 1999**
Santiago, Dominican Republic

United States Map

The Astros play in Houston, Texas.

World Map

What's in the Locker?

Baseball teams wear different uniforms for home games and away games. Houston's home uniform is bright white. It has thin, black stripes called pinstripes. The uniform top spells out **A-S-T-R-O-S** in script.

Michael Bourn wears the team's home uniform.

Houston's away uniform is gray with no pinstripes. The uniform top spells out **H-O-U-S-T-O-N**, in script. The players wear a cap with a star on it.

Carlos Lee wears the team's road uniform.

21

We Won!

The dream of every baseball team is to reach the World Series. In 2005, the Astros finally made it there. Their fans had waited for 43 years!

The Astros started slowly that season. Then they started winning game after game. They won more times than any other team the rest of the season. Houston fans will never forget the year that their Astros were champions of the National League.

The Astros win again in 2005.

Record Book

These Astros stars set amazing team records.

Hitter	Record	Year
Roger Metzger	14 Triples	1973
Jeff Bagwell	.368 **Batting Average**	1994
Craig Biggio	210 Hits	1998

Pitcher	Record	Year
Dave Roberts	6 **Shutouts**	1973
Billy Wagner	44 **Saves**	2003
Jose Valverde	44 Saves	2008

Answer for ABC's of Baseball

*Here are words in the picture that start with **H**: Head, Helmet, Heel, Hop, Hunter Pence, Houston Uniform. Did you find any others?*

Answer for Brain Games

The first fact is true. Jose Cruz Jr. played for nine teams, including the Astros in 2008. Jose Cruz was an Astro for 13 years, but he never hit a ball out of the Astrodome.

Baseball Words

BATTING AVERAGE
A measure of how often a batter gets a hit. A .300 average is very good.

RUNS BATTED IN
The number of runners that score on a batter's hits and walks.

SAVES
A number that shows how many times a pitcher comes into a game and completes a win for his team.

SHUTOUTS
A number that shows how many times a pitcher goes an entire game without giving up a run.

Index

Photos are on **bold** numbered pages.

About the Astros

Learn more about the Astros at houston.astros.mlb.com

Learn more about baseball at www.baseballhalloffame.org